WHY TRUMP IS A GREAT LEADER

& DESERVES RESPECT

HENRY WASHINGTON PHD

WHY TRUMP IS A GREAT LEADER

WHY TRUMP IS A GREAT LEADER

WHY TRUMP IS A GREAT LEADER

WHY TRUMP IS A GREAT LEADER

WHY TRUMP IS A GREAT LEADER

WHY TRUMP IS A GREAT LEADER

WHY TRUMP IS A GREAT LEADER

WHY TRUMP IS A GREAT LEADER

WHY TRUMP IS A GREAT LEADER

WHY TRUMP IS A GREAT LEADER

WHY TRUMP IS A GREAT LEADER

WHY TRUMP IS A GREAT LEADER

WHY TRUMP IS A GREAT LEADER

WHY TRUMP IS A GREAT LEADER

WHY TRUMP IS A GREAT LEADER

WHY TRUMP IS A GREAT LEADER

WHY TRUMP IS A GREAT LEADER

WHY TRUMP IS A GREAT LEADER

WHY TRUMP IS A GREAT LEADER

WHY TRUMP IS A GREAT LEADER

WHY TRUMP IS A GREAT LEADER

WHY TRUMP IS A GREAT LEADER

WHY TRUMP IS A GREAT LEADER

WHY TRUMP IS A GREAT LEADER

WHY TRUMP IS A GREAT LEADER

WHY TRUMP IS A GREAT LEADER

WHY TRUMP IS A GREAT LEADER

WHY TRUMP IS A GREAT LEADER

WHY TRUMP IS A GREAT LEADER

WHY TRUMP IS A GREAT LEADER

WHY TRUMP IS A GREAT LEADER

.

WHY TRUMP IS A GREAT LEADER

WHY TRUMP IS A GREAT LEADER

WHY TRUMP IS A GREAT LEADER

WHY TRUMP IS A GREAT LEADER

.

WHY TRUMP IS A GREAT LEADER

WHY TRUMP IS A GREAT LEADER

WHY TRUMP IS A GREAT LEADER

WHY TRUMP IS A GREAT LEADER

WHY TRUMP IS A GREAT LEADER

WHY TRUMP IS A GREAT LEADER

WHY TRUMP IS A GREAT LEADER

WHY TRUMP IS A GREAT LEADER

WHY TRUMP IS A GREAT LEADER

WHY TRUMP IS A GREAT LEADER

WHY TRUMP IS A GREAT LEADER

WHY TRUMP IS A GREAT LEADER

WHY TRUMP IS A GREAT LEADER

WHY TRUMP IS A GREAT LEADER

WHY TRUMP IS A GREAT LEADER

WHY TRUMP IS A GREAT LEADER

WHY TRUMP IS A GREAT LEADER

WHY TRUMP IS A GREAT LEADER

WHY TRUMP IS A GREAT LEADER

WHY TRUMP IS A GREAT LEADER

WHY TRUMP IS A GREAT LEADER

WHY TRUMP IS A GREAT LEADER

WHY TRUMP IS A GREAT LEADER

WHY TRUMP IS A GREAT LEADER

WHY TRUMP IS A GREAT LEADER

WHY TRUMP IS A GREAT LEADER

WHY TRUMP IS A GREAT LEADER

WHY TRUMP IS A GREAT LEADER

WHY TRUMP IS A GREAT LEADER

WHY TRUMP IS A GREAT LEADER

WHY TRUMP IS A GREAT LEADER

WHY TRUMP IS A GREAT LEADER

WHY TRUMP IS A GREAT LEADER

WHY TRUMP IS A GREAT LEADER

WHY TRUMP IS A GREAT LEADER

WHY TRUMP IS A GREAT LEADER

WHY TRUMP IS A GREAT LEADER

WHY TRUMP IS A GREAT LEADER

WHY TRUMP IS A GREAT LEADER

WHY TRUMP IS A GREAT LEADER

WHY TRUMP IS A GREAT LEADER

Made in the USA
Las Vegas, NV
14 September 2024

95272138R00056